Presented to

....

From

....

DON'T WORRY ABOUT
Tomorrow

Illustrations by Susan Reagan

Melody Carlson

Broadman & Holman Publishers B&H Nashville, Tennessee

Text copyright © 2001 by Melody Carlson

Illustration copyright © 2001 by Susan Reagan

Cover and interior design: Uttley/DouPonce DesignWorks

Published in 2001 by Broadman & Holman Publishers,
Nashville, Tennessee

Scripture taken from the HOLY BIBLE,
NEW INTERNATIONAL VERSION ®, copyright © 1973,
1978, 1984 by International Bible Society. Used by permission
of Zondervan Publishing House. All rights reserved.

A catalog record for this book is available
from the Library of Congress.

All rights reserved. Printed in Korea.

ISBN 0-8054-2386-9

1 2 3 4 5   05 04 03 02 01

Don't Worry About Tomorrow

Do you ever get worried or all full of fear?

Do you fret that tomorrow your bed won't be here?

Do you imagine that bad things may lurk at your door,

That your roof may fly off — in the rainstorm will pour!

You may think I'm silly or off in my head,

Because I was anxious and so full of dread.

But then I learned something that changed everything,

And now I'm so happy I can't help but sing!

It happened one day at my grandfather's farm.

I hid in the house to keep safe from all harm.

When Gram said, 'go play,' I just had to refuse,

"If I go outside, I might spoil my new shoes."

Gram patted my head, and then said to me,

"Look out the front window, and what do you see?"

I looked in her garden to see spiders and bugs,

And next to the rosebush, a couple of slugs.

"I see lots of dirt and some things that are creepy."

And then I yawned big, but I was not sleepy.

"Look higher," she said. "See the birds and the flowers.

They never worry, they play by the hours."

Gram gave me a hug, then she walked away,

While I watched the birds and the flowers at play.

The birds did look glad as they frolicked about.

"Come out here and join us!" Did I hear them shout?

Then I forgot all about my new shoes,

And went to the garden, I couldn't refuse.

And here's where my story goes out on a limb.

Instead of being me, I became one of them!

I know it's incredible, how could it be so?

(It was all just a dream, I thought you should know.)

But out of my shoulders popped two little wings,

I hopped on a branch and my feet felt like springs.

"What happened?" I asked a small chickadee.

"I feel like a bird and yet I'm still me!"

The chickadee laughed, and just flipped her tail,

She said, "Just follow me," and off we did sail!

Flying was easy until I looked down.

"My goodness!" I shrieked when I saw the ground.

"What if I fall?" I asked my bird friend.

"A fall from up here would mean it's the end!"

She giggled with mirth, saying, "Don't be afraid.

We have wings to fly. It's how we are made."

I flew and considered all I had heard,

I thought I could learn a lot from this bird.

Soon I grew hungry from flying around.

I wondered where my next meal might be found.

I asked my new bird friend (hope it wasn't rude)

"Where is the place where you birds keep your food?"

She laughed and she said, "There is plenty for all.

God provides for each of us, both big ones and small."

Then she dove from the sky to a huge cherry tree.

Where the cherries were juicy, and they were for free!

My tummy was full as we sailed through the sky.

"A bird's life is cool," I said with a sigh.

She nodded and said, "Yes, birds do have fun.

We sleep in the night and we sing in the sun.

We've never a worry," she said as she landed.

"Never?" I asked. "I just don't understand it."

She looked at me funny and then cocked her head.

"Don't you trust your Maker?" is all that she said.

Down in the garden I thought on her words.

It seems trust comes easy for chickadee birds.

But what is it like for the posies and pansies?

Do they fret for rain? Have wild flower fancies?

Then it happened again! I know it sounds silly,

But I was transformed right into a lily!

My feet became roots planted deep in the ground,

My face turned to petals, I suddenly found.

Being a lily was really quite nice.

The smell from my blossom

was better than spice.

And quickly I learned just how little they toil.

Their face to the sun; their feet in cool soil.

I looked at the rosebush, she seemed so content,

No need for a roof and she never paid rent.

Could it be true that she hadn't a care?

What if drought threatened, would that bring a scare?

And what about winter with wind and with snow?

What happened then and where would she go?

"Excuse me, dear Rose?" I asked my new friend.

"Do you ever worry that summer might end?"

Then Rose leaned toward me, a smile on her face,

And said, "Me worry? In this lovely place?

God made the whole world, and He takes care of me,

Giving water and sunshine — the beauty you see."

I said, "It sounds good, but it's hard to accept,

I've gotten so used to my worries and fret."

"You worry?" said Rose, "Doesn't God love you too?

Doesn't He always take good care of you?"

So through a red rose and a small chickadee,

My Father above taught a lesson to me.

He says, "Do not worry and fret for your life."

And now I'm not filled with such fear and such strife.

I know that God loves us — loves us one and all.

He gives what we need whether we're great or small.

And if I forget where I found this new power,

I simply remember the birds and the flowers!

Do not worry about your life

Look at the birds of the air

See how the lilies of the field grow

Taken from MATTHEW 6:25-32